EDGE
BOOKS

THE KIDS' GUIDE TO

BUILDING COOL stuff

by Sheri Bell-Rehwoldt

Capstone
press®

Mankato, Minnesota

Edge Books are published by Capstone Press,
151 Good Counsel Drive, P.O. Box 669, Mankato, Minnesota 56002.
www.capstonepress.com

Library of Congress Cataloging-in-Publication Data
Bell-Rehwoldt, Sheri.
    The kids' guide to building cool stuff / by Sheri Bell-Rehwoldt.
    p. cm.   (Edge books. Kids' guides)
    "Provides instructions for building a variety of fun, simple projects using
household materials"   Provided by publisher.
    Includes bibliographical references and index.
    ISBN-13: 978-1-4296-2276-9 (hardcover)
    ISBN-10: 1-4296-2276-8 (hardcover)
    1. Handicraft   Juvenile literature. 2. Amusements   Juvenile literature.
3. Science   Experiments   Juvenile literature. I. Title.
TT160.B4556 2009
745.5   dc22   2008029687

Editorial Credits
Christopher L. Harbo, editor; Bobbi J. Wyss, designer;
    Marcy Morin, project production

Photo Credits
Capstone Press/Karon Dubke, 5 (top), 18 (bottom)
Capstone Press/TJ Thoraldson Digital Photography, (all project steps)
Shutterstock, cover

Printed in the United States of America in Stevens Point, Wisconsin.

022010
005705R

Table of Contents

INTRODUCTION

Do you need to spice up a Saturday afternoon? Are you and your friends itching to build something? Well, look no further. The pages of this book are packed with projects you can put together.

But where will you get the materials you need? Believe it or not, your house is probably loaded with stuff that can become your next cool project. Is there an empty milk carton in the recycle bin? Turn it into a bird feeder. Do you have aluminum foil and a paper cup? A bubbling volcano is waiting to be born.

Nothing is more satisfying than making something with your own hands. The project doesn't have to be hard to build or have a million parts. It just has to be cool enough to make you proud that you built it.

The projects in this book will get your brain thinking and your hands creating. You can make them on your own, or have your friends help out to double the fun. Just remember to ask an adult to help when you need to use box cutters, hot glue, and other dangerous tools.

What are you waiting for? Let's get started!

Paper Boat

Got water? Then you need a boat! Fortunately, with just a page of newspaper, you can quickly make your own. Happy sailing, mate!

What You Need

* double-spread newspaper page

Step 1: Rip the newspaper page in two down the long middle seam.

Step 2: Fold the paper in half.

Step 3: Fold the paper in half again and unfold.

Step 4: Fold the top corners to the center crease.

Step 5: Fold the top layer of the bottom edge.

Step 6: Fold the corners behind the model and turn the model over.

Step 7: Fold the bottom edge as you did in step 5.

6

Step 8: Slide your thumbs into the model and pull the triangle open. Press the model into a diamond shape.

Step 9: Fold the top layer to the point and turn the model over.

Step 10: Fold the remaining layer to the point.

Step 11: Open and press the model into a diamond shape as you did in step 8.

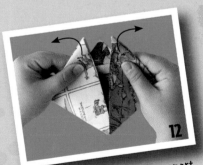

Step 12: Pull the two points apart. Spread apart the bottom of the model to help the boat stay open.

Your boat is now ready to sail!

Impressiveness: ★☆☆   **Complexity:** ★☆☆

BUBBLING VOLCANO

What You Need

* tape
* paper snack cup
* paper plate
* aluminum foil
* scissors
* cookie sheet with raised lip
* 2 tablespoons (30 mL) of water
* red food coloring
* 1 tablespoon (15 mL) of baking soda
* 2 tablespoons (30 mL) of white vinegar

What's all that bubbling and frothing? It's just your very own erupting volcano! Build this, and your friends will be over in an instant to see all the action.

1 & 2

3

Step 1: Tape the bottom of the paper cup to the center of the paper plate.

Step 2: Cover the cup and plate with a long piece of foil. Make it long enough to fold around the edges of the plate.

Step 3: Use scissors to poke a hole in the foil where it covers the center of the cup. Cut four slits from the hole to the edges of the cup to create tabs. Fold the tabs down and tape them inside the cup.

Impressiveness: ★★★   **Complexity:** ★☆☆

Step 4: Set your volcano on a large cookie sheet. Pour the water into the cone of the volcano. Then add several drops of red food coloring and the baking soda.

Step 5: Pour in the vinegar and watch your volcano erupt!

Note: The volcano erupts because the vinegar and the baking soda have a chemical reaction. The vinegar is an **acid** that reacts with the baking soda to make a froth.

« **acid** a substance that tastes sour and that can burn your skin »

FIZZLE ROCKS

What You Need

* spoon
* 1/4 cup (60 mL) of water
* 1 cup (240 mL) of baking soda
* food coloring
* small mixing bowl
* small plastic toys
* plate
* 4 cups (960 mL) of white vinegar
* large, clear bowl

Can rocks dissolve? These rocks do. And your friends will think the prizes hidden inside them are super cool!

Step 1: Use a spoon to mix the water, baking soda, and a couple drops of food coloring together in the mixing bowl. A stiff dough should form. If it seems too wet, add more baking soda. If it seems too dry, add more water.

Step 2: Scoop a spoonful of the dough into the palm of your hand. Press one of your prizes into the dough. Roll the dough around in your hands until it looks like a rock. Be sure to use enough dough to hide the prize.

Impressiveness: ★★☆   **Complexity:** ★★☆

Step 3: Place each finished rock on the plate. Put the plate in a safe place overnight so the rocks have time to dry and harden.

Step 4: When you're ready to surprise your friends, pour the vinegar into the clear bowl. Then gently drop one of your rocks into the vinegar.

Step 5: Watch your friends stare in amazement as the dough fizzles away to nothing. All that's left behind are the hidden prizes!

VINEGAR LAUNCHER

What You Need

* cork
* plastic soda bottle
* tape
* paper towel
* 1 teaspoon (5 mL) of baking soda
* toilet paper
* funnel
* white vinegar
* water
* safety glasses

What can you make with a soda bottle and a couple of ordinary baking ingredients? A really cool rocket! With a good, hard shake, your rocket will head for the sky!

Step 1: Bring all of your items to a safe outdoor area away from people. Make sure the cork fits snugly into the neck of the bottle. If it doesn't, wrap tape around the cork until it does.

Step 2: Rip the paper towel into 1-inch (2.5-centimeter) strips. Tape the strips to the top of the cork. These strips will help you see the cork when it launches.

Step 3: Pour the baking soda into the center of one square of toilet paper. Then carefully fold the square so that you have a tidy little packet. Set aside.

Step 4: Place the funnel in the neck of the bottle. Pour about a half-inch (1.3 centimeters) of vinegar into the bottle. Then pour in enough water to fill the bottle about half full.

Step 5: Put on your safety glasses. Carefully point the bottle away from you and your friends. Drop the baking soda packet into the bottle. Then firmly wedge the cork into the bottle. Give the bottle a hard shake. Quickly place the bottle on the ground and stand back.

Whooooosh! Watch your cork rocket blast into the air.

Impressiveness: ★★★   **Complexity:** ★★☆

BALLOON ROCKET

What You Need

* 15-foot (4.6-meter) piece of fishing line
* plastic drinking straw
* 2 sturdy chairs
* hot dog-shaped balloon
* tape

Balloons aren't just for birthday parties. They can be rockets in disguise. Build a zip line and get ready to blast off!

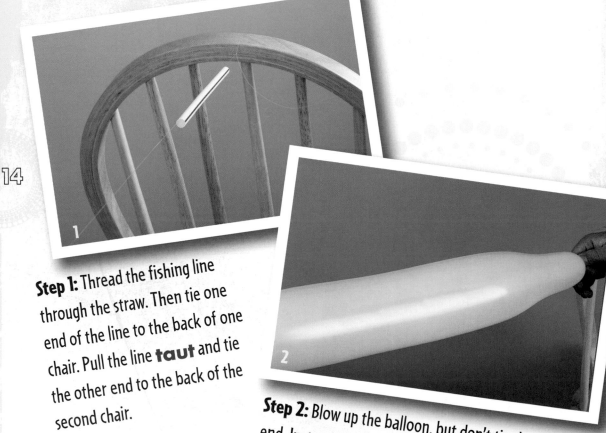

Step 1: Thread the fishing line through the straw. Then tie one end of the line to the back of one chair. Pull the line **taut** and tie the other end to the back of the second chair.

Step 2: Blow up the balloon, but don't tie the end. Instead, pinch or twist the end to keep the air from escaping.

« **taut** stretched tight »

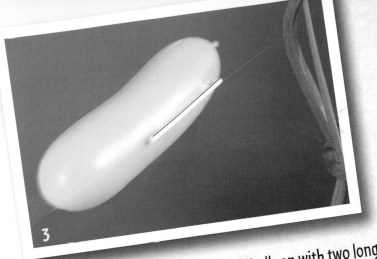

TIP: INCREASE YOUR FUN BY MAKING ROCKET LINES FOR YOUR FRIENDS. THEN COMPETE TO SEE WHOSE BALLOON BLASTS OFF THE FASTEST.

Step 3: Tape the straw to the top of the balloon with two long pieces of tape. Make sure the closed end of the balloon is facing a chair.

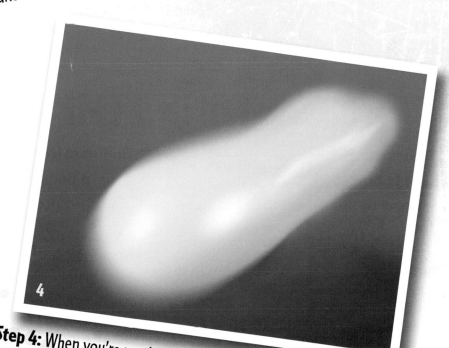

Step 4: When you're ready for your rocket to blast off, let go of the pinched end of the balloon. It will zoom down the fishing line on your air power!

Impressiveness: ★★☆   **Complexity:** ★☆☆

MILK CARTON BIRD FEEDER

What You Need

- ★ stapler
- ★ empty half-gallon (1.9-liter) cardboard milk carton
- ★ hole punch
- ★ ruler
- ★ pencil

- ★ utility knife
- ★ 12-inch (30-centimeter) wooden dowel
- ★ brown or green nontoxic poster paint
- ★ paintbrush

- ★ wooden craft sticks
- ★ hot glue gun
- ★ twine
- ★ birdseed

Are you looking for a recycling project to help the planet? Here's one that will make the birds in your neighborhood very happy.

16

Step 1: Staple the opened lip of the milk carton shut. Then use a hole punch to make a hole in the center of the carton's top edge. You will hang the bird feeder from this hole.

Step 2: Lay the carton on its side. Measure 5 inches (13 centimeters) from the top of the carton and mark this spot with a pencil. Then measure 8 inches (20 centimeters) from the top of the carton and mark this spot too. Have an adult use the utility knife to cut a square between the two lines. Leave about a half-inch (1.3 centimeters) on the left and right edges of the cut.

Step 3: Turn the carton over and repeat Step 2. You now have openings on two sides for birds to use.

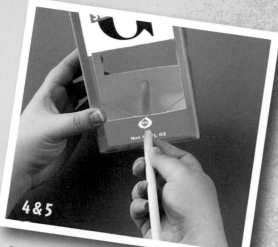

4 & 5

Step 4: Punch a hole about 1 inch (2.5 centimeters) below the square opening with the hole punch. Slide the wooden dowel through the hole until it butts up against the other side of the carton. Mark an "X" where you feel it hitting the carton. Punch a second hole here.

Step 5: Slide the wooden **dowel** through both holes. The dowel should stick out evenly on both sides. Birds now have a perch to rest on while they're eating.

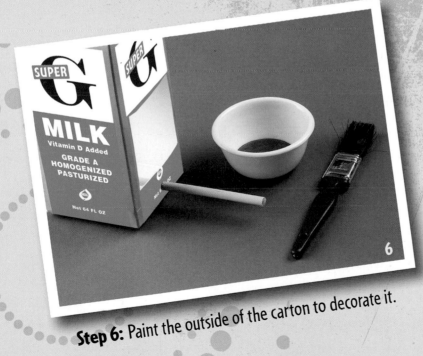

6

Step 6: Paint the outside of the carton to decorate it.

PROJECT CONTINUED ON PAGE 18 ▶▶▶

« **dowel** a long, thin piece of wood »

7 & 8

Step 7: Attach the craft sticks to the top of the feeder with the hot glue gun. Paint the roof green.

Step 8: Loop twine through the hole you made in the top of the feeder.

18

TIP: YOU CAN MAKE BIRD FEEDERS FOR SMALLER BIRDS BY USING THE MILK CARTONS YOU GET AT SCHOOL.

Pour birdseed into the bird feeder. Hang it in a tree and your birdy café is open for business!

FLY HIGH KITE

What You Need

* 24-inch (61-centimeter) wood dowel
* 20-inch (51-centimeter) wood dowel
* utility knife
* tape measure
* pencil
* kite string
* scissors
* heavy-duty plastic trash bag
* packing tape
* large sewing needle
* twine
* ribbon

Are you looking for a windy-day activity? Make a kite. Ben Franklin did it and so can you.

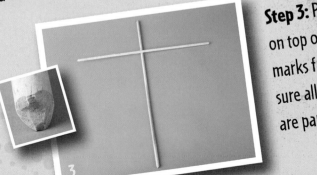

Step 1: Ask an adult to cut a notch in each end of the dowels with a utility knife.

Step 2: On the longer dowel, use your tape measure and pencil to mark a line that is 6 inches (15 centimeters) from one end. On the shorter dowel, mark a line that is 10 inches (25 centimeters) from the end.

Step 3: Place the short dowel on top of the long dowel so the marks from step 2 cross. Make sure all the notches in the tips are parallel with the table.

PROJECT CONTINUED ON PAGE 20 ▶▶▶

19

Impressiveness: ★★★   **Complexity:** ★★★

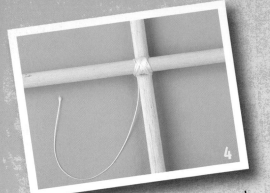

Step 4: Wind the kite string around the dowels where they cross. As you wind the string, make an "X" pattern around the sticks until they are bound tightly together. Make sure the notches stay parallel to the table. Leave about 5 inches (13 centimeters) of the string hanging freely.

Step 5: Pull the roll toward the end of one of the dowels. Thread the string through the notch in the dowel. Then continue winding the string through the other three notches. Wind the string around the outside of the kite one more time. Make sure the string is tight.

Step 6: Pull the string to the center of the kite and wrap it around the X a few more times. Then cut the string off the roll, leaving about 5 inches (13 centimeters) free. Tie this end tightly to the other free end from step 4.

Step 7: Place the kite frame on top of the trash bag. Cut the bag around the kite, leaving several inches on all sides. Fold these edges over the sides of the kite frame and tape them down. Add more tape to the top and bottom tips of your kite to strengthen these areas.

Step 8: Cut a 2-foot (.6-meter) piece of string. Use the sewing needle to thread the string through the plastic and around the dowels at the top and bottom tips of the kite. Tie the ends of the string together. This string is called a bridle.

Step 9: Tie your kite string about one-third of the way down the bridle. You can move the knot higher or lower later if the kite has trouble flying.

Step 10: For the tail, tape a 6-foot (1.8-meter) piece of twine to the bottom point of your kite. Then tie ribbon down the length of the twine to give your kite extra stability.

Fly your kite on a breezy day in an open field or park.

SUNNY DOG

What You Need

* cardboard oatmeal canister and lid
* pencil
* aluminum foil
* scissors
* hole punch
* tape
* 10-inch (25-centimeter) wooden skewer
* hot dog

Think you need a gas grill to cook a hot dog? You don't if the sun is shining. This cooker will roast your dog with the sun's intense solar rays.

Step 1: Use the lid from the oatmeal canister and a pencil to trace two circles on a piece of foil. Cut the circles out and set aside.

Step 2: Cut the canister lid in half. Set aside.

Step 3: Cut the canister in half lengthwise. Place one of the lid halves on the open end of one of the canister halves.

Step 4: With your hole punch, make holes through the center of the lid and the canister bottom.

Impressiveness: ★★☆　　　**Complexity:** ★★☆

Step 5: Wrap the foil circles from step 1 over the ends of your cooker and tape them in place.

Step 6: Cut a long piece of foil to fit into the middle of the cooker. Gently press the foil into the canister so it becomes a second skin. Wrap the extra ends around the outside of the cooker.

Step 7: Poke the skewer through the hot dog. Push the ends of the skewer through the foil and holes at the ends of the cooker. Put the cooker in the sun. Angle it so the sun's rays **reflect** off the foil. The reflected light will heat up your hot dog. Turn the skewer to rotate the hot dog for even heating.

« **reflect** to bounce off an object »

HOVERCRAFT

What You Need

* disposable plastic plate
* Phillips screwdriver
* 35-mm film canister
* poster putty
* balloon

This simple hovercraft is made from just a few household items. But it really zooms! Send it hovering across the table on a cushion of air.

1 & 2

Step 1: Poke a hole in the center of the plate with a screwdriver.

Step 2: Use your screwdriver to poke another hole in the center of the bottom of the film canister. This will take a bit of muscle power.

3

Step 3: Press poster putty around the open edge of the film canister. Then turn it over and press it directly over the hole in the plate.

Impressiveness: ★★☆   Complexity: ★★☆

4 & 5

Step 4: Blow up the balloon, but don't tie the end. Instead, twist the balloon about 1 inch (2.5 centimeters) from the end to keep the air from escaping.

Step 5: Wrap the open end of the balloon over the film canister. Don't let go of the twist yet!

When you're ready for takeoff, set the plate down on a flat, smooth table. Let go of the balloon twist and flick the plate with your fingers. It will zoom across the table as the air shoots out of the balloon.

WATER BRIDGE

What You Need

* large liquid measuring cup
* water
* blue food coloring
* 2-foot (.6-meter) piece of rope
* bowl
* tape

Here's a challenge for you. Try building a rope bridge that allows water to flow from a measuring cup to a bowl. Even better, challenge a friend to see who can finish the project first.

Step 1: Find a spot outside. Fill the measuring cup with water. Add a few drops of food coloring. Then dunk the rope in the measuring cup to get it wet.

Step 2: Place the bowl on the ground. Tape the bottom end of the rope inside the bowl. Place the other end of the rope across the measuring cup and over the spout. Hold the end of the rope with your thumb.

Step 3: Hold the measuring cup up in the air, away from the bowl, until the rope between them is taut. The rope will be at an angle, as shown.

TIP: IF YOU SET UP TWO WATER BRIDGES, YOU AND A FRIEND CAN RACE TO SEE WHO CAN GET THE MOST WATER INTO THE BOWL THE FASTEST.

Slowly tip the measuring cup so the water in the cup begins to trickle down the rope. When you get the hang of it, the water from the measuring cup will end up in the bowl. Until then, expect to get a bit wet!

Impressiveness: ★★☆   **Complexity:** ★☆☆

GOT BUTTER?

What You Need

* 1 cup (240 mL) of heavy whipping cream
* glass jar with lid
* kitchen timer
* knife
* salt (optional)
* chives or dill (optional)
* fresh bread

With just a little cream and a jar, even city slickers can make their own butter. But be warned, you might want to buff up your arm muscles first. Making butter is a real workout.

Step 1: Pour the whipping cream into the jar. Screw the lid on the jar tightly. You're about to give the jar the shaking of a lifetime!

Step 2: Set the timer for 10 minutes and shake the jar **vigorously**. As you shake, you'll see the fat and protein inside the liquid begin to clump together. Keep shaking and the clump will grow bigger and bigger.

« **vigorous** energetic, lively, or forceful »

Step 3: When the buzzer goes off, you should have a glob of butter and a little bit of liquid. Pour any remaining liquid out of the jar.

Use the knife to pull the butter out of the jar. Taste it. If you want to make it saltier, mix in a dash of salt. Keep adding more salt a bit at a time until it tastes right. You can also add fresh herbs such as chives or dill. Spread the butter on some bread and serve.

Impressiveness: ★★☆   **Complexity:** ★★☆

GLOSSARY

acid (ASS-id) — a substance that tastes sour and that can burn your skin

dowel (DOW-ul) — a long, thin piece of wood

parallel (PA-ruh-lel) — two straight lines that stay the same distance from each other and never cross or meet

reflect (ri-FLEKT) — to bounce off an object

taut (TAWT) — stretched tight

vigorous (VIG-ur-uhss) — energetic, lively, or forceful

Buchanan, Andrea J., and Miriam Peskowitz. *The Daring Book for Girls.* New York: Collins, 2007.

Iggulden, Conn, and Hal Iggulden. *The Dangerous Book for Boys.* New York: Collins, 2007.

O'Sullivan, Joanne. *101 Things You Gotta Do Before You're 12!* New York: Lark Books, 2007.

Internet Sites

FactHound offers a safe, fun way to find educator-approved Internet sites related to this book.

Here's what you do:

1. Visit *www.facthound.com*
2. Choose your grade level.
3. Begin your search.

This book's ID number is 9781429622769.

FactHound will fetch the best sites for you!

INDEX

ABOUT THE AUTHOR

Sheri Bell-Rehwoldt considered herself a crafty kid. But she freely admits she wasn't the sharpest tool in the shed when it came to power tools.

Sheri is an award-winning author. She has written numerous children's books, including *You Think It's Easy Being the Tooth Fairy?*